101 Things I Learned in Product Design School

101 Things I Learned® in Product Design School

Sung Jang and Martin Thaler with Matthew Frederick

CROWN
NEW YORK

Published in the United States by Crown, an imprint of Random House, a division of Penguin Random House LLC, New York.

CROWN and the Crown colophon are registered trademarks of Penguin Random House LLC.

Library of Congress Cataloging-in-Publication Data
Names: Jang, Sung, author. | Thaler, Martin, author. | Frederick, Matthew, author.
Title: 101 things I learned in product design school / Sung Jang and Martin Thaler with Matthew Frederick.
Other titles: One hundred one things I learned in product design school
Description: First Crown edition. | New York: Crown, an imprint of Random House, a division of Penguin Random House LLC, [2020] | Series: 101 things I learned | Includes index.
Identifiers: LCCN 2020007233 (print) | LCCN 2020007234 (ebook) | ISBN 9780451496737 (hardcover) | ISBN 9780451496744 (ebook)
Subjects: LCSH: Product design.
Classification: LCC TS171 .J37 2020 (print) | LCC TS171 (ebook) | DDC 658.5/752—dc23
LC record available at https://lccn.loc.gov/2020007233
LC ebook record available at https://lccn.loc.gov/2020007234

Printed in China

randomhousebooks.com

Illustrations by Sung Jang, Matthew Frederick, and Martin Thaler
Cover illustration by Sung Jang and Matthew Frederick

9 8 7 6 5 4 3

First Edition

Authors' Note

You may have picked up this book because you are studying product design, have an idea for a product, or are simply interested in how products are conceived, made, marketed, and sold.

Product design is an enormous field. Products are everywhere, serving vastly different needs, functioning in highly variable contexts, and answering to markedly different aesthetic sensibilities. The key to designing successfully over such a broad spectrum is a foundation in core principles. In our experience, these principles often go unarticulated in the design curriculum. And so we have prepared the following lessons in plain language with simple drawings, in an effort to demonstrate the universal bases, philosophical underpinnings, and technical essentials that will help get you started in this complex, fascinating field. We hope they make you a more informed designer, and that you will return to them again and again.

Sung Jang and Martin Thaler

Acknowledgments

From Marty and Sung

Thanks to Craighton Berman, Karen Choe and family, Dale Fahnstrom, David Gresham, Chris Hacker, TJ Kim, Ed Koizumi, Richard Latham, Stephen Melamed, Bill Moggridge, Peter Pfanner, Zach Pino, Craig Sampson, Lisa Thaler and family, Scott Wilson, and Robert Zolna.

From Matt

Thanks to Carla Diana, Sorche Fairbank, Matt Inman, James Lard, Jorge Paricio, and Erik Tuft.

101 Things I Learned in Product Design School

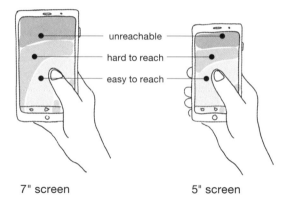

unreachable

hard to reach

easy to reach

7" screen   5" screen

Design is a physical act.

Design requires deep reflection, but one cannot design in a purely cognitive (thinking) mode. Active doing helps us figure out what to think about. Otherwise, we think only about the things we already know.

All design is done in relation to the body, so one must use the body to design. Even virtual/digital products engage the body through visual interface, touch screens, and pointing devices. Bias the design process toward action, using your own body as a tool. Act out the user experience. Pretend to push the button. Operate the control screen. Sit in the chair prototype as a user of the real chair would.

Entice

Enter

Engage

Exit

Extend

After the 5E customer journey model by Larry Keeley

You're always designing within a system.

A system is a set of interconnected things; each thing is related to and inter-dependent with the others. When designing anything, think several increments outward into the many systems related to the product. If designing a paper cup, investigate the manufacturing, distribution, retail, and use systems. If designing an electronic device, consider the complex digital ecosystem within which it will likely reside. Consider the product's temporal context—the sequence of events and user behaviors before and after it is engaged. Consider the infrastructure that may be needed to support a new product; a great idea isn't a great idea without a support system in the real world.

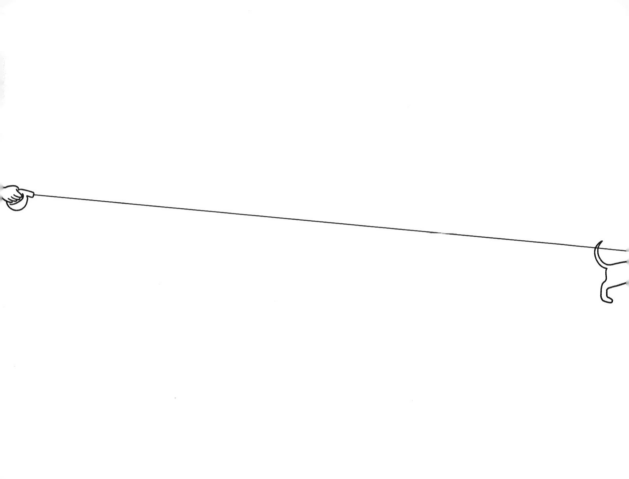

The apparent problem probably isn't the real problem.

An apparent problem is usually a symptom of an underlying macro-problem, and sometimes of an entirely different issue. For example, you might be asked to design a better pooper-scooper because people aren't picking up after their dogs. A reasonable assumption might be that this is because people don't want to risk touching excrement. But research might reveal that owners simply forget to take bags on their walks. A new scooper would not solve this problem, so the problem must be **reframed** as one of placing bags where dog walkers need them—perhaps within the leash handle, in a dispenser at the dog park, or at key locations on city streets.

If a problem is too abstract, ask *what*.
If it's too specific, ask *why*.

Too abstract: You have been charged with reducing customer service response time but have not been told which practices, procedures, equipment, etc., on which to focus.

Ask *what:* What is the tangible evidence of the problem? What has the client previously done to address it? What are the particular goals of employee activities? What procedures and equipment are being used? Which are essential and which are not?

Too specific*:* You have been asked to design a bicycle headlight.

Ask *why*: Why is a new light needed? Is it for riders to see where they are going? Is it to make them more visible to others? Is it for a specific kind of bike or riding environment? Is it because of new battery technology? Is it because the company's existing design is no longer up to date?

Jaywayne USB Cool Mist Humidifier

A need is a verb.

People don't need a vase; they need to display and enjoy flowers. They don't need a teacup; they need to consume tea. They don't need a chair; they need to experience rest. They don't need a lamp; they need lighting. They don't need a humidifier; they need to humidify the air. They don't need a water bottle; they need to drink liquid while on the move. They don't need a parking garage; they need to store their car. They don't need a library ladder; they need to access information.

CDs

Secondary products

food

coffee beans

Core product

coffee

tumbler

mug

Identify the experience, not just the product.

Every product has one or more core experiences that transcend the product itself. The core experience of mountain biking may be biking, but it also could be exploring the outdoors, embracing physical challenge, or escaping worka-day structure. Identifying the core experience clarifies users' motivations and needs. This can lead not only to better design responses, but to developing secondary products for the same user—perhaps rain gear, emergency tools, and high-nutrition snacks. These products may build additional interest in the core experience and increase users' reliance on the product brand.

Originality isn't Step One.

Originality doesn't begin with originality, but with developing basic competencies. Copying the works of the masters will build your visual awareness and physical skills and help you learn the essential workings of things. For any one exercise, establish a narrow set of goals. Use the same medium as the original you are copying whenever possible. Duplicate all details. Focus on being persistent, consistent, and repetitive. Don't worry about expression; the time spent learning a skill is not a time to be creative.

Mastering and internalizing skills will eventually unleash creativity by allowing you to direct your conscious efforts toward your ideas rather than the physical process of depicting them.

Automatic

higher cost
perpetual operation
sweeping second hand

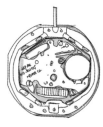

Quartz

lower cost
battery operation
ticking second hand

Internal watch movement

Learn how everything works *conceptually*, if not *technically*.

Conceptual understandings grasp the basic principles of how a thing functions, the ways it works within or among systems, its general look and feel, and the user's experience of it. They dwell on the big picture *why*, and less on the detailed *how*.

Technical understandings address the literal workings of something, such as mechanics, material properties, tolerances, and manufacturing methods. Technical thinking is often compartmented and may focus on only one part or portion of a system rather than the overall system, and rarely if ever the *why* behind the system's existence.

Begin with familiar objects.

Trying to attract people to something entirely new is risky. A radical product almost always calls for more time, financial investment, and testing than an incrementally improved product. And it may be impossible to poll consumers on its potential value to them because they lack a relevant comparison.

But consumers can give useful feedback on incremental improvements to familiar products. **Archetypes** have gone through a period of evolution that makes them enduring and comfortable. When improved, they are more likely to be integrated into users' lives. The Nest thermostat, for example, is based on the ubiquitous Honeywell thermostat, but it incorporates sustainable materials as well as technology that learns users' heating and cooling preferences. A more expressive shape signifying its advanced technology might have been more exciting, but the familiar shape reassures consumers and fits more naturally into their homes.

Common
table lamp

Sisifo lamp
by Scott Wilson

Common
task lamp

Novel, but not too novel. Familiar, but not too familiar.

Scientific studies show that an animal typically reacts with fear when encountering a new stimulus. Subsequent, repeated exposures are usually met by curiosity, active investigation, and sometimes fondness or friendship. Our reaction to inanimate objects is shaped by this same instinct of defense and survival. Although a new, very novel product is unlikely to prompt fear, it may engender visceral dislike, such that consumers avoid it. The narrow market window for many new products means it may fail before consumers adapt to it.

Designer Raymond Loewy advocated for the **MAYA principle:** products that are Most Advanced Yet Acceptable balance the comfort of the familiar with the stimulation of the unfamiliar, encouraging consumers to accept a new object into their familiar world.

iPod by Jonathan Ive

"It's very easy to be different, but very difficult to be better."

—JONATHAN IVE

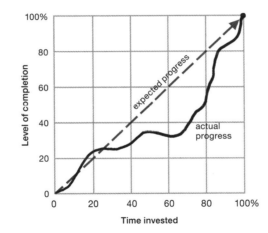

Creativity is nonlinear.

It is common and even typical for an inexperienced designer to come up with a solution quickly, stick to it, and defend it against criticism by invoking a right to be creative and self-expressive. But this actually indicates an avoidance of creativity and self-expression. To be creative is not to execute a preconceived idea; it is to continually learn, discover, and try out new possibilities. It is to pursue vulnerability—to embrace not knowing what to do, to actively place oneself in situations that require one to create something unexpected.

How to make a blank sheet of paper less scary

Few things offer as much promise or are as intimidating as a blank sheet of paper. But if you tear it in half, it's half as scary. Tear it into a quarter sheet, and draw two lines or write three words. Use a thick marker, which will force you to focus on the essence of your ideas. Soon you will be on your way to brainstorming, defining user scenarios, or organizing a presentation.

Make your ideas mobile.

Being creative isn't just coming up with new ideas; perhaps more often it's *connecting* ideas. The more a designer can freely move among ideas, the more likely important connections will materialize. Posting your drawings, research notes, lists, and brainstorms on a wall or whiteboard makes multiple ideas visible at once, maximizing the likelihood of identifying useful, novel connections. If connections aren't evident, mush the materials around. Rearrange, cluster, organize, combine, uncombine, manipulate, and reinterpret them to generate new patterns, ideas, user scenarios, and narrative sequences. Invite others into the process to multiply opportunities.

Design needs language.

Each week, write a design statement—a paragraph explaining your understanding of the users, the problem, and your approach. Don't record only fully formed ideas; use your writing as a tool for thinking and discovering, and for refining old understandings you may have thought settled. Don't hesitate to spend an hour on a single paragraph if needed.

When you encounter major obstacles in the design process or are stymied by a looming decision, review an accumulation of design statements to see if their evolution suggests a natural next step.

People move public chairs before sitting in them.

Observation

This seems significant in some way.

Awareness

This is how people assert choice and control, and create defensible space!

Insight

Inspired by the observations of William H. Whyte, *The Social Life of Small Urban Spaces*

An insight is more than an observation.

An **observation** is the perception of an objective fact or condition. An **awareness** is an observation that continues to reside in the mind, carrying with it an expectation of significance. An **insight** is the recognition of the deep significance of something one already knew. An insight is revelatory and holistic; it organizes complex relationships or ambiguous phenomena in a simple, clarifying way.

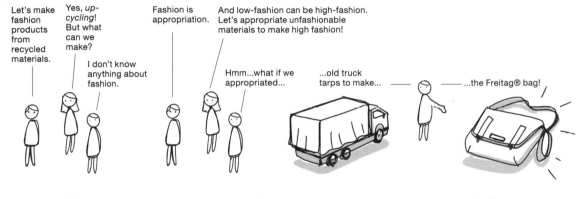

A concept is more than an idea.

An **idea** is an original thought that may or may not be of significant or lasting value. A **concept** is broader and more powerful: it derives from an elemental insight into human nature or behavior and applies to the product secondarily. A concept is both strong and nuanced. It implies a product's form, its aesthetic sensibility, and the feelings a user will likely have in engaging it.

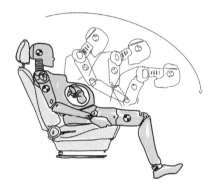

A 50th percentile man is not a 50th percentile human.

Women and men have different body chemistries and respond differently to medication. But the default subject for medical research is a 155 lb. male. Google software recognizes male speech with 70% greater accuracy than female speech. Standard workplace temperatures are based on male metabolism, making an average office five degrees too cold for women. Goggles, harnesses, and other safety gear are based on male anatomy. Women can select a smaller size, but must accept critical proportional differences.

The US government began using crash test dummies in 1950, based on a 50th percentile male. Women drivers, who sit more upright and closer to the wheel, were deemed "out of position" and were not tested or designed for. They are 47% more likely than men to be seriously injured in accidents. A "female" dummy was introduced in 2011; it was a scaled-down male dummy.

Sympathy
an intellectual or abstract recognition of another's feelings
without feeling the same way

Empathy
an emotional reaction to
another's situation; feeling
another's feelings for oneself

Turn sympathy into empathy.

Twenty-six-year-old designer Patricia Moore wanted to create products anyone could use. She conducted an experiment to learn the realities of life for an 80-year-old woman. She plugged her ears, wore glasses that blurred her vision, and clipped on a leg brace to impair her walking.

Upon venturing into the urban environment, she found that many things she had taken for granted were designed with only the young and healthy in mind. Her studies and subsequent proposals led to innovations that have become commonplace, such as low-floor and "kneeling" buses, ramped curb cuts, and signage with large type. Many of the changes, although intended for the disabled, benefit the able-bodied. Curb cuts for wheelchairs, for example, assist people pushing shopping carts and baby strollers, as well as bicyclists and skateboarders transferring between sidewalk and street.

Diverge: possibilities expand through research, inquiry, brainstorming, exploration, and generation of concepts

Converge: possibilities narrow through synthesis, discarding of unworkable ideas, development of more focused solutions

Front-load the design process.

Technical progress tends to be more tangible than design progress: it's very difficult to design the right solution, and fairly easy to technically execute many solutions. This can make it tempting to decide quickly on a solution and move it into technical development. But before becoming invested in a solution, budget lots of time for fuzzy, conceptual explorations and daydreaming. Work open-endedly without pursuing practical outcomes. Go down roads that appear to not lead anywhere. If you're designing a frying pan, set aside a couple of weeks to flip pancakes, sketch open-endedly, and hack prototypes. Don't ignore hard research and structured methods, but don't think about molds, parts, and costs too soon.

 ≈

 ≈

Explore the product personality early.

When someone encounters the product, what feelings should it evoke? What senses will be engaged? How should they feel when they see, touch, or use it? What fond experiences might it lead them to recall? What is the product's inner character? Should it be stolid, dependable, mysterious, lighthearted, aggressive, self-contained, flighty, fancy, retro, clunky, or understated? What scale and proportion will feel right? What colors, textures, shapes, and patterns are suggested? What sizes and types of controls, buttons, hardware, and other interaction points are called for? Is it traditional or cutting edge? What values will the user look for—safety, solidity, high-fashion, femininity, invisibility, technological innovation? What metaphors help describe the experience of using the product? What will stand out in repeated uses? How might the satisfied user describe the product to others? What is the personality of the intended users, and what identity keys can be borrowed from them to make it feel right?

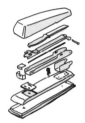

Do some *how* work with *why* work and some *why* work with *how* work.

22

The earlier parts of the design process focus heavily on *why* work: Why are users experiencing a pain point? Why aren't existing solutions adequate? Why might Scheme A be of greater value than Scheme B?

As the design process matures, it focuses more on *how* a solution may be realized—by considering precise dimensions, mechanical and electronic workings, material types and thicknesses, details, fastenings, finishes, and manufacturing methods.

Why work and *how* work, if distinct, are nonetheless interdependent. Whenever a *why* exploration suggests a potential solution, momentarily walk it into the *how* phase to test its viability, then return to more *why* work. Likewise, during the *how* phase, return frequently to the essential *why* questions to inform technical resolution.

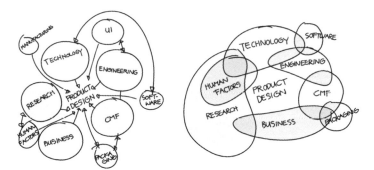

Multidisciplinary team

Interdisciplinary team

It's better to violate a boundary than to leave a gap.

23

Design is inherently interdisciplinary, not multidisciplinary. Decisions made by any part of a team affect all others.

Program manager: establishes and defines project scope; manages overall process and schedule; coordinates meetings; monitors budgets.

Marketing manager: represents the company's brand values; analyzes existing products; conducts tests to assess consumer interest, market size, and price.

Engineer: ensures a product will be functional to use, feasible to produce, and will be delivered on schedule.

Researcher: investigates opportunities in the market; conducts interviews and secondary research to gain insights into consumer concerns and values.

User Interface (UI)/User Experience (UX) designer: designs experiences between people and products or services, often through digital interfaces.

Business strategist: defines a project's financial goal and its impact on the company.

Product designer: synthesizes research findings, marketing, branding, manufacturing requirements, etc., in designing a product.

Tapered base:
- eases release from manu-facturing mold
- facilitates stacking of parts
- provides visual and physi-cal stability
- tilts interface screen toward user

Rounded corners:
- are pleasant to touch
- are structurally stronger than right-angle corners
- provide pleasing visual "softness"

24

Form follows function . . . and much else.

Modernism is **functionalist:** it posits that a form exists to serve a function, and that any forms and embellishments lacking utility are to be discarded. But while function may be the most critical consideration in design, there are many factors to which a product and its features must answer, regardless of philosophy. The more factors a design decision responds to, the more successful the outcome will likely be.

Three ways to conceptualize form

25

Additive forms appear to have been made by assembling, attaching, agglomerating, or intersecting parts. They tend to have a mechanical aesthetic. A classic film camera is an example.

Subtractive forms appear to have been made by removing material, for example a wood product shaped by a lathe. They tend to be highly unified in appearance.

Morphed forms appear to have been shaped by applying force, such as pushing or pulling, to a starting form. They often look organic. An example is a bicycle seat.

Some forms literally express how they were made, but many do not. A vase with a morphed form might have been produced by 3-D printing (an additive process), computer numerical control milling (a subtractive process), or a combination of the two.

Taj Mahal, Agra, India

Random hypothesis: Beauty is universal.

26

Objects considered beautiful by one culture are almost always considered beautiful by other cultures. Yet the objects produced by any one culture are often very different from those made by another culture. Some cultures produce sensuous, earthy forms; others value the austere and high tech. Some value decorative embellishment, while others prefer unadorned surfaces. Some emphasize rectilinear shapes, others the curvilinear.

If cultures hold similar ideas of beauty, why do such differences exist? It is because *other* factors—the display of power or prestige, historical references, physical context, and more—also shape how things look, and cultures value these factors in different proportion. The aesthetic outcomes are very different, even though notions of beauty are very similar.

Sign value

Utility value

Casio: $10

Patek Philippe: $80,000

A $25 teakettle needs to boil water, whistle, be dependable, and look appealing. A $900 kettle mostly needs to be beautiful.

27

The cost of a tangible function tends to be apparent in a market economy. A $10 Casio watch, for example, is almost purely functional, thereby establishing that telling time has a **utility value** of perhaps $9. A Patek Philippe watch can cost $80,000, suggesting that almost all of its value is **sign value**—the status it grants its wearer. Prestige, being an abstract quality, lacks a clear price standard.

E-reader

Make it look like what it does.

28

A well-designed product communicates how it is to be engaged through **affordances**—cues as to how to hold, use, or otherwise interact with it. Affordances build on a user's mental models of the action to be performed. Rotate the knob and pull to open the door. Grasp a teapot by the handle and pour from the spout on the opposite side. Flip a switch up to turn on and down to turn off.

Affordances often build on users' past experiences. When soda cans changed from a detachable to an attached latch, consumers had to relearn how to open a can, but they still knew where to open it. Identifying affordances for a global product can be challenging, as they may vary across cultures. Squat-style toilets in China, for example, are not typically understood by Westerners.

Camel table by Richard Neutra

Emulate nature's functions, not its forms.

29

Many innovations model nature. Velcro, the looped fastener, models the way seeds attach themselves to passing animals to spread to new places to grow. The field of **biomimicry** seeks to understand nature's complexity and replicate it in designed objects. But don't confuse this with literally copying shapes found in nature. Emulate a natural object's structural and functional properties, not its specific visual form.

Short-stemmed glass by Joe Cesare Colombo, 1964

Question tradition, but don't dismiss it outright.

30

Does a wineglass need a stem? Designer Karim Rashid argues it is a pointless artifact from centuries ago, when tall-stemmed metal goblets signaled social status. To maintain it, he argues, is to ignore the user's real needs. In a turbulent airplane, for example, does it make sense for a flier to drink wine from a stemmed glass?

But in many contemporary contexts, a stemmed glass still seems superior. Its graceful form suits the special occasions at which wine is often served. For those toasting, stemmed glasses properly "clink." Even left on a table, a stemmed glass allows light to shine through the elevated body. Indeed, a stemless glass can adequately hold wine, but a stemmed glass *presents* wine.

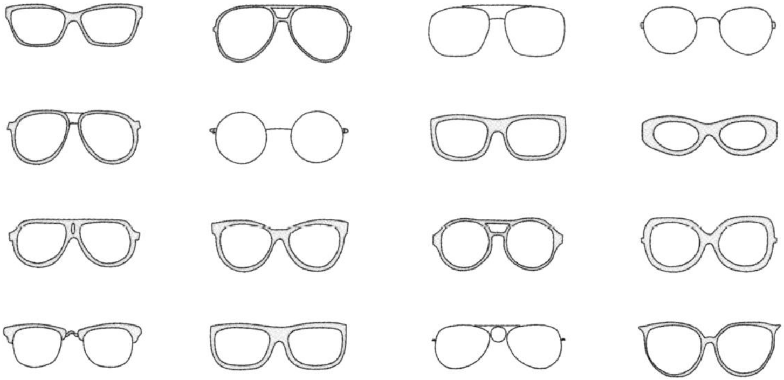

Shapes are loaded.

Shapes have deep histories and carry embedded meanings. Very slight differences in their execution can fundamentally alter how a product is understood, its historical and cultural references, and the audience that embraces it.

31

The earliest eyeglasses of the 13th century were purely functional, and thus had round lenses. Later, when other shapes were introduced as fashion items, round lenses acquired meanings tied to their functional roots. Figures as diverse as John Lennon, Steve Jobs, and Mahatma Gandhi embraced them to convey simplicity, directness, learnedness, asceticism, and spiritualism—and to show, perhaps, how to reject fashion fashionably.

Aviator sunglasses were developed in the 1930s for airplane pilots as a replacement for uncomfortable goggles. Their success is due to their lightness, a convex profile, and a simple shape that closely covers the eye socket. Prominent WWII news photos of General Douglas MacArthur turned them into mainstream symbols of adventure.

Traditional design

tends to celebrate visual
complexity; forms are
often created through
addition or agglomeration

Modern design

tends to simplify and unitize;
forms may conceal complexity
to achieve outer simplicity and
facilitate mass manufacture

Elegance is the opposite of extravagance.

Elegance is a phenomenon of aesthetic efficiency. An elegant form seems minimal but embodies sophistication and complexity. **Extravagance** displays complexity through an accumulation of features, embellishments, and details. Although conceptual opposites, elegance and extravagance do not have a binary relationship. Elegance is not the stripping away of extravagance, as one can create a minimal form that is inelegant.

Both elegance and extravagance are relevant design strategies that offer aesthetic opportunities—and dangers: a failed attempt at extravagance may result in cluttered garishness, while failed elegance may appear simplistic and dull.

Korean pottery often displays subtle, intentional asymmetry to create both tension and comfort.

Dissonance is desirable.

Potter Pete Pinnell collects mugs by other artists. He liked the earthy character of a mug by Linda Christianson, but a ridge on the handle dug into his finger, and the rim was rough on his lips. Frustrated, Pinnell put the cup away.

Some time later, he tried it again. On the second audition, Pinnell realized that the mug's dissonant qualities forced him to consciously notice each sip. He lamented the many cups of tea he had consumed absentmindedly over the years, "without even tasting them."

Pinnell credits this experience with changing his understanding of art: "Sometimes, something that's completely resolved isn't as interesting. . . . A little bit of dissonance, at least a little bit, is really required to have an interesting composition that will hold our interest over a long period of time."

breast pocket lining
inverts to become
pocket square

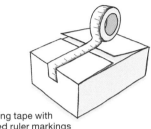

packing tape with
printed ruler markings

Lego key chain allows
easy attachment and
detachment

Cleverness is unexpected efficiency.

Cleverness prompts delight, but it is fundamentally a functional, not emotional, quality. It engages and rewards by offering a solution or detail that is multifaceted but unexpectedly simple. It solves a core functional problem while adding at least one more element of functional value.

A gimmick may lend initial delight, but will likely fail in the longer run because it adds little or nothing of functional value. Gimmickry asks to be noticed; cleverness does not ask to be noticed but is noticed anyway.

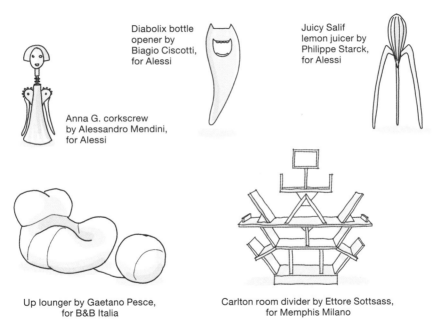

Diabolix bottle opener by Biagio Ciscotti, for Alessi

Juicy Salif lemon juicer by Philippe Starck, for Alessi

Anna G. corkscrew by Alessandro Mendini, for Alessi

Up lounger by Gaetano Pesce, for B&B Italia

Carlton room divider by Ettore Sottsass, for Memphis Milano

A playful object doesn't have to be an object for play.

Playful forms work best when introduced into ordinary, familiar products, such as those commonly found in the home and office. This is because their function is well understood, limiting the potential for confusion.

When seeking playfulness, see if the product's inherent form suggests anything. References should be whimsical, not cute or kitschy. Simplify the form to avoid literalism: most people will be more comfortable using a handsaw that vaguely suggests a cat than using a literally rendered cat whose ability to cut wood is not evident in its form. Use natural features and details in the referenced object, such as eyes and limbs, to support the product's functions. Finally, use high-quality materials to assure the user that the product isn't a gimmicky throwaway.

35

A toy doesn't have to be cute.

The Radio Flyer is an object for children's play. But the form of the "little red wagon" is not inherently playful. Introduced in the 1930s and still manufactured today, the stamped metal body is rugged and industrial. Large corner radii make it safer to play with. Black rubber wheels with big white metal hubs make for smooth rolling. Operation is easily understood: load up the wagon and pull it, or get in and steer it down a hill.

A well-executed children's product doesn't need to have a "Disney narrative" attached to it. Contrived imagery or styling may increase sales temporarily, but will ultimately limit appeal and date a product, and licensing fees will make it more expensive.

36

Camp knows; kitsch doesn't.

campy: intentionally exaggerating familiar themes or qualities, resulting in a deliberately absurd or wryly humorous tone.

cheesy: lacking authenticity or subtlety; calculated to elicit a particular response from an audience, usually by overstating or telegraphing intent.

kitsch: art or objects with a naive, garish, or sentimental aesthetic that "knowing" individuals may deem of poor taste but may appreciate ironically, e.g., a lava lamp or pink flamingo lawn decoration.

schlocky: of low quality.

tacky: overtly seeking to display fanciness, wealth, or status while belying a lack of sophistication or refinement.

taste: an individual's aesthetic sensibility; it may be shaped by knowledge, personal bias, experience, security, education, and class identity.

trite: unoriginal and overused, thereby being of little or no value.

twee: affectedly or cloyingly pretty, picturesque, quaint, or sentimental.

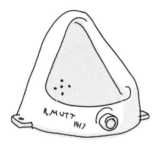

Fountain, by Marcel Duchamp, 1917

The camera created modern art.

Historically, visual art was both representational and expressive: it aimed to depict the world realistically as well as convey the artist's subjective intent. Because the camera can depict reality very accurately, its invention "stole" one-half of art's traditional role. Art responded by becoming oriented to expression over representation. Soon it turned its eye on itself, asking: What is art, anyway? Must paint be applied with a brush? Is a work of art fixed and final, or should it continue to change? Must art tell a coherent story or be conventionally beautiful? Must art be lofty, or can it depict the prosaic? And to the extent art depicts reality, what does "real" really mean?

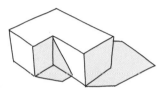

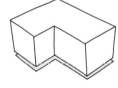

Realistic shadow

harder to draw and
usually unnecessary

Symbolic shadow

drop the object's bottom plane
to quickly convey depth

Draw as a designer, not as an artist.

Draw efficiently, not expressively. Most drawings should be quick, clear visitations of ideas, not precious pieces of art.

Draw symbolically, not realistically. Omit peripheral details to bring focus to the message you want the viewer to receive.

Don't strive for a signature drawing style. Let your personal style develop organically over time.

Draw fast. The computer is for detailed renderings. In hand sketching, rapid visualization is most important; it communicates ideas in conversation.

How to draw a straight line

Use a felt pen. If drawing long lines, use a thicker pen for greater presence, as a more prominent line is easier to evaluate.

Draw individual lines slowly. If you stroke a line too quickly, you will have less control over direction and straightness.

Move your entire arm rather than pivot from the elbow. Drag your drawing hand across the page if it adds traction.

Slightly wiggly lines are okay as long as the overall line is straight and not an arc.

Rotate the drawing medium if it makes it easier to draw straight lines.

Don't "flick" the line. Give the start and end a hard stop.

Repeat until you are able to draw consistently straight lines with a clear beginning and end. This will take at least a few weeks of moderate training to internalize into muscle memory.

Strong perspective
dynamic, but
distorting

Mild perspective
accurate, but less
"personality"

Use perspective drawings for expression. Use orthographic drawings for investigation.

Perspective sketches are effective for capturing an overall idea quickly, and may make a strong impression by showing a product's relationship to space or its use context. But **orthographic drawings** (two-dimensional plans, sections, and elevations) are much more likely to help you evolve an idea. Their inherent exactness, especially when drawn full size, compels a designer to investigate and pursue specific decisions on size, scale, proportion, and detail.

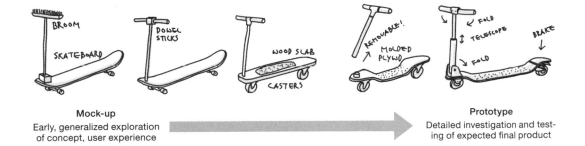

BROOM
SKATEBOARD

DOWEL STICKS

WOOD SLAB
CASTERS

REMOVABLE!
MOLDED PLYWD

FOLD
TELESCOPE
FOLD
BRAKE

Mock-up
Early, generalized exploration of concept, user experience

Prototype
Detailed investigation and testing of expected final product

Drawings simulate appearance.
Mock-ups simulate experience.

An artistically rendered drawing can look great, have emotional impact, and provide a snapshot of a product's visual character and appeal. But only a mock-up (typically, a rough, three-dimensional study) or prototype (usually a closer approximation of the expected final product) can place you in the mode of using the product.

Cut foam board in 3 passes

1. Top skin
2. Foam
3. Bottom skin

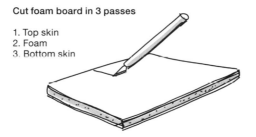

Mock up to discover, not just depict.

Seek to answer specific questions. A mock-up or prototype should help you confirm or refute a speculation. A failed prototype can still succeed: by revealing a problem, it shows you what does not work and suggests where you should go next.

Seek to discover new questions. Your goal shouldn't be to build a perfect version of an idea, but to place yourself in a situation that prompts you to ask questions you otherwise would not have thought of.

43

Build at full scale. This allows you to test the product's presence in space, its usability, and its relationship to the body. If a full-scale study is not practical in three dimensions, a full-scale, two-dimensional drawing will sometimes suffice.

Build rough. An early "Frankenprototype" can consist of found objects taped together to simulate a general experience.

Limit the number of elements. Minimize time and expense by focusing on key explorations. As the design advances, studies should become more complex.

All products move.

Portability is critical, even for products that remain stationary in ordinary use. A large, heavy printer may sit in the same place for years, but indentations built into the sides will be appreciated when it is set up and on the rare occasions when it must be moved. A home refrigerator has wheels on the bottom and a mattress has handles on the side, even though they will remain stationary for most or all of their lives.

A product moves again when its useful life is complete and it is disassembled, thrown away, or recycled.

44

Archive
product in
storage

Anticipated
product in use context
but not performing

Active
product performing
core function

Use modes

Products perform when not in use.

When is a credenza "in use"? When it is placed in a living room or office, at the moment an object is placed in or on it, or when it sits idle?

Indeed, many products are at work when not performing their primary function. Furniture, lighting fixtures, dishes, and countless other products serve as background or aesthetic objects, or simply stand at the ready, when not being actively operated.

The ultimate effectiveness of a product may depend on its **context** (manufacture, transport, display, installation, storage, disposal, etc.) more than its **primary use** (its ordinary, intended function or application). A window air conditioner can be designed to run efficiently, but its true efficiency depends on the integrity of its installation. A headphone should be designed for the wearer's comfort, but its value to the user may hinge on whether it can be folded for transport and storage.

45

General modules

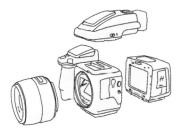

Specialized modules

Make anything approximately or a few things perfectly.

Modules are multiple, standardized units used to construct a complete object. They allow high flexibility and mobility for the user and efficiency in design, engineering, production, and inventory for the manufacturer.

General modules can be assembled into almost any shape, from a castle to a whale. However, each assembly will be an approximation. Any object made with Lego modules, for example, will look like a Lego-based approximation of the intended object.

Specialized modules allow a narrow range of outcomes, but each outcome closely serves a specific need. Hasselblad, for example, builds modules that allow one to compose a variety of cameras. Office furniture and kitchen cabinet modules can be combined similarly.

handspan
usu. 7" to 9"

chair
seat 18"±
above floor

table
30"± above
floor

1 gallon
6" x 6" x 6" ±

11 sticky notes
1mm ±

Understand your world in numbers.

Make a habit of guessing the dimensions of objects in your environment, then measure them to see how close you were. Measure the dimensions and spacing of controls and buttons. Measure your eye height in a seated position, and the ratio of television screen size to preferred viewing distance. Measure the spaces between parked cars and between icons on a phone screen. Measure the size of a soda can, cell phone, dollar bill, house key, paperback book, air conditioner, dinner plate, and Shih Tzu.

47

A 200-pound person isn't twice the size of a 100-pound person.

Volume and mass are deceptive. The ideal size, shape, visual character, and ergonomics of a three-dimensional form can be assessed only by prototyping it at full scale and seeing and using it in its intended context. Even a half-scale prototype deceives: while it may seem close enough to actual size to evaluate, its volume is only *one-eighth* that of a full-scale model.

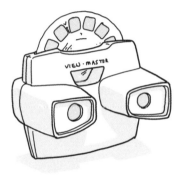

GAF View-Master by Charles Harrison, 1958

10% thicker is 33% stronger.

Consumers tend to perceive material stiffness as an indicator of overall product quality. For most materials, a modest 10% increase in thickness will yield an impressive one-third increase in strength and stiffness, reducing twisting, housing squeaks, "oil canning," and other structural problems and annoyances.

49

3 point base
for quick set-up
and leveling

4 point base
for stability of
stationary objects

5 or 6 point base
for stability of
rolling objects

Recognize the gravity of the situation.

We know intuitively that an object that is narrower at the top than the bottom has a lower center of gravity and is less likely to tip than an untapered object. Our sense of visual stability derives from this understanding, as even objects that are not vulnerable to tipping, such as a traditional lampshade, are often more visually satisfying when made narrower at the top.

A disposable coffee cup may seem to overlook gravity in that it is wider at the top, which facilitates pouring into it, drinking from it, and stacking it. This makes it more prone to tipping than is desirable. Yet gravity still drives the cup's form: when you hold it, gravity pulls the cup down into the semicircle formed by your thumb and fingers. If the cup were wider at the bottom, it would be very difficult to hold.

A product has a right weight.

In furniture, heaviness may be perceived as a sign of quality. In a laptop computer it may convey the opposite. Lightness may suggest efficiency in a headphone but cheapness in a frying pan. A heavy-soled dress shoe will usually feel of high quality, but a good athletic shoe will feel light and lithe. A portable stapler should be light, but a stationary stapler should be hefty. A disposable pen should be light, while a fountain pen should be heavy to convey durability and gravitas. Disposable razors are lightweight, suiting them to travel, but razors for home use are heavy and more lasting.

Floor lamp by Isamu Noguchi

"It is weight that gives meaning to weightlessness."

—ISAMU NOGUCHI

Attached/standardized hinge
doesn't express or
augment concept

Physically integrated hinge
may or may not
relate to concept

Conceptually integrated hinge
inseparable from
product concept

Details *are* the concept.

Details are not just about the small areas in a product. They are opportunities to manifest the design intent. If a concept aims for smooth minimalism, round the corners, hide seams and fasteners, and use flush buttons. If a concept aims for a constructed sensibility, compose the forms additively, use different colors, finishes, or materials for the different parts, employ exposed fasteners, and exaggerate joints with deep reveals or other embellishment.

Work detail-toward-concept as well as concept-toward-detail: if a detail can't be executed to help the concept, it's probably telling you to reconsider the concept.

53

A box is more than a box.

A product housing is made of at least two parts. The **parting line** that separates them may be located by purely practical concerns, such as internal workings, manufacturing ease, or structural strength. But other locations can communicate a message. Placed on the bottom of a product, a parting line is concealed during ordinary use, communicating solidity—a desirable trait in a stationary product. Bringing it to the top may showcase precise assembly. Placing it at midpoint on the sides is neutral or generic, but may provide an opportunity to visually enliven the product by using different colors or finishes on the two housing pieces.

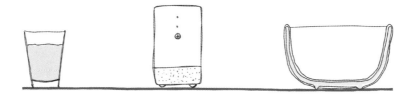

54

Paper cup
sides extend for
stability, allow
bottom to sag

Electronics
rubber feet assist
ventilation, minimize
housing "buzz"

Ceramics
feet keep raw
clay from sticking
to kiln surface

Use your feet.

Many products need feet to help them stand level, but feet can be functional in other ways. They can provide grip, prevent scratching of the product bottom, absorb impacts, protect the surface on which the product sits, improve performance, make visual sense of the form, and even assist in its manufacture.

55

Slotted

can suggest retro "throwback," but may look generic

Allen/hex

suggests ruggedness

Torx/star

small; suggests precision

Phillips/cross

practical, but may look generic

Use your heads.

Screw heads can be hidden behind labels or rubber feet. But when exposed, they can communicate important messages about a product's concept or the brand identity.

56

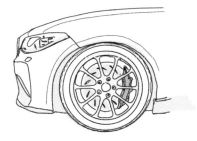

Brembo brake caliper

Go partial Monty.

If a product contains complex components or innovative technology, consider making it visible from the outside to express high performance. But keep it subtle. Give a small hint rather than go full Monty.

57

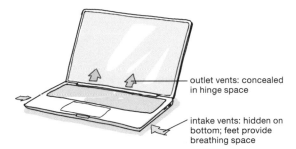

outlet vents: concealed in hinge space

intake vents: hidden on bottom; feet provide breathing space

Air in, air out.

Passive ventilation: For a product that generates a modest amount of heat, such as a television, radio, or kitchen appliance, provide openings in the housing to promote natural air movement through the product.

Active ventilation: When a product contains internal components that generate substantial heat, integrate a fan to move air from an intake vent across to an outlet vent.

Forced ventilation: For a product whose primary function is to move air, such as a room fan or hair dryer, design the intake and outlet vents to prevent the insertion of fingers and hair.

Ventilation as a design feature: A laptop computer may be expected to convey effortless computation, suggesting concealed intakes and outlets. But vents might be emphasized on a gaming laptop to signify its robustness. Air movement is the central purpose of a room fan, yet Dyson's avant-garde fans conceal this function to draw attention to their unique shape.

Color as utility

makes an important
thing easy to locate

Color as symbol

conveys excitement,
satisfaction

Color as audience identifier

may convey gender, social status,
fashion, political affiliation

Color starts with non-color.

Every material has an inherent color. Work with it before introducing other colors. Use color to serve a clear purpose: as a function, such as highlighting points of interaction; as an audience or brand identifier; or to suit the environment in which it will be used.

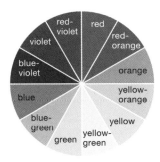

Hue
spectrum of color

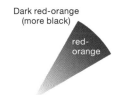

Dark red-orange
(more black)

red-orange

Light red-orange
(more white)

Tone or value
lightness or darkness
of a hue

Light tones amplify details. Dark tones amplify silhouette.

Lighter tones naturally reveal variations in light and shadow, suiting them to objects whose contours and details are meant to be appreciated, such as classical marble statues. It is more difficult to perceive variations and details within darker tones, suiting them to objects that are not meant to be noticed, such as staplers, mouse pads, and living room electronics.

An exception is the automobile, because a glossy, dark surface in a bright outdoor setting acts as a mirror. The many reflections on a dark car make its form look more complex and contoured than the same model of car in white.

60

White is practical. Black is sophisticated. Metal is professional.

White is a natural choice for products in which purity, cleanliness, and utility are valued, making it the default color for laundry and kitchen appliances ("white goods"). Black tends to imply sophistication, especially for personal products such as leather goods. This is in part because it obscures surface details, lending an air of mystery.

Metal finishes such as brushed stainless steel tend to project a professional vibe. Homeowners wishing to convey professional-level capability within their homes are increasingly favoring it for new appliances.

61

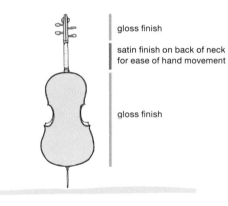

gloss finish

satin finish on back of neck
for ease of hand movement

gloss finish

Satin is more slippery than gloss.

Rough surfaces tend to have more "grip" than smooth surfaces, making our hands and feet more steady and secure. But when smoothness increases beyond a certain point, this ceases to be the case. Gloss, the smoothest possible finish, has more grip than a satin finish.

62

Natural color enhanced by surface treatment

polishing
sandblasting
clear coating

Color infused into material

dyeing or staining, or mixing pigments into material during casting

Layer of color technically bonded

chemical, electrostatic, electrolytic, or thermal process

Paint is a last resort.

Products whose finish reveals, rather than conceals, the material's true color tend to command higher value and age better than products with a painted surface. Paint wears, chips, and fades in ways that degrade a product. It can be an effective cover for cheap materials, but it may also advertise that the underlying material is cheap: if it *isn't* cheap, why is it hidden?

63

RGB

use to select and
specify colors for
screen use

CMYK

use to select and
specify colors for
physical objects

Pantone

proprietary system for
specifying colors for
print, paint, plastics

Mold-Tech

proprietary system for
selecting texture and
finish of plastics

Use physical samples to make physical decisions.

For physical products, don't trust a computer screen to select colors, materials, and finishes (CMF). Refer instead to physical industry standards such as those from Pantone and Mold-Tech. However, even when following these standards, different manufacturers may produce different results, and a specified color may look different on different materials or finishes. Reviewing physical production samples from the manufacturer is the best way to select and confirm CMF.

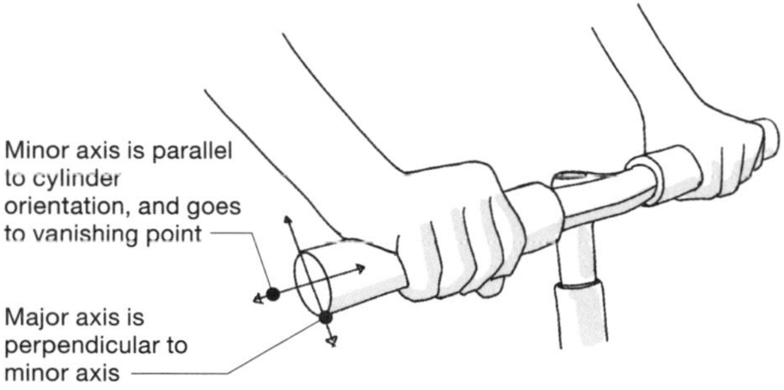

Minor axis is parallel
to cylinder
orientation, and goes
to vanishing point

Major axis is
perpendicular to
minor axis

A circle in perspective is an ellipse.

Good ergonomics doesn't necessarily mean a perfect fit.

A sculpted shape that fits the hand closely can provide extraordinary initial comfort. But it may not prove optimal in extended use, as its conformance may restrict movement and adjustment; there is only one way to engage it. By comparison, a cylinder provides less initial comfort but allows the user to freely shift positions. It also may be more manufacturable and less expensive than an ergonomically "correct" device.

65

Lying

Reclining
socially aware,
not socially
engaged

Casual
socially aware,
informally
engaged

Upright
socially en-
gaged, socially
focused

Task
focused,
individualized
activity

Bar height
sociable;
short-term
commitment

Standing

Seating principles

The lower you sit, the longer you sit, and the greater the role of comfort.

Backrests and armrests imply greater commitment; e.g., a backless bench implies shorter-term use than a dining chair or lounger.

Right angles inhibit comfort. A seating surface should usually be lower at the rear edge than at the front, producing a tilt up to 5° from horizontal. A backrest should slope backward 5° to 15°.

Swivel indicates performance/utility, e.g., a task chair, barstool.

More upright tends to suggest greater social engagement. Greater reclination suggests greater privacy. A recliner in a public space, such as a beach or movie theater, exhibits an atypical mixture of private posture and public experience.

Table height = elbow height of a seated person.

66

Wassily chair by Marcel Breuer, 1925

"A chair is the first thing you need when you don't really need anything, and is therefore a peculiarly compelling symbol of civilization. For it is civilization, not survival, that requires design."

—RALPH CAPLAN,
By Design

67

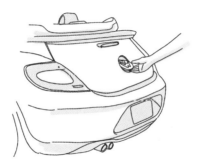

Volkswagen trunk release

Give the user a fair chance to figure it out.

Providing users an opportunity to discover a feature is different from hiding a feature. Annoyance will likely result when the user is both visually and physically barred from easy or intuitive access—for example, when a power button is located on the back of a speaker. But a pleasant *aha!* may result when the user has an opportunity to discover a feature that is not initially apparent but is nonetheless accessible, such as a product logo that turns out to be the power button. Once users recognize it, there is no further barrier to use. They may think "Why didn't I see this before?" and enjoy reliving their original *aha!* on subsequent uses.

68

The greater the consequence, the more physical the switch.

Flush buttons have minimal physical presence and usually require direct visual access. They suit functions used occasionally, such as submenu programming. They effectively preserve the purity of a product's form, but are difficult to find by feel.

Extruded buttons are raised slightly; one can find them by feel. They often suit common operations, such as "Scan" or "Paper feed." A particularly high extrusion may be appropriate for the primary operation of a device, e.g., "Puree" on a blender or "Record" on a video camera.

Recessed buttons suit special, seldom-used functions whose accidental activation could be catastrophic. They are often made deliberately difficult to press, such that special physical effort must be made. Activating "Reset" on a Wi-Fi router, for example, may require the insertion of a pen tip or paper clip.

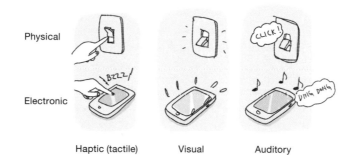

69

Types of feedback

Did what was supposed to happen happen?

Some products provide automatic feedback: a vacuum cleaner unmistakably communicates that it has been turned on or off. But users of many products need additional cues to discern if an intended interaction has taken place.

Work across the sensory spectrum to determine the best cue for the user context. Visual cues, such as LEDs, are common, but **haptic** (touch) feedback is often more effective. For example, a vibration may be more effective than a visual cue for indicating a cell phone has been placed in silent mode. In an especially busy visual context, such as a computer screen or automobile dashboard, an auditory cue may be most readily noticed. A multi-note melody can distinguish between turning on (ascending notes), changing modes (same/similar notes), and turning off (descending notes).

70

Windows

An unknown error occurred

If the problem persists, restart program.
Check online Help for solutions

⌃ Hide details   Restart   Close

Error code: 12345

Software is unavoidably imperfect.

Consumers expect physical products to be perfect or near perfect. But software users are comparatively accepting of imperfections. They may be annoyed by bugs and shortcomings, but they will work around them until an update is issued. At that point, they likely will expect—and receive—fresh features in addition to fixes. This will result in a new round of imperfections that they will accept and work around.

A software company, therefore, has little incentive to work out every bug in a product before putting it on sale. If it were to take more time to do so, consumers would not wait, but would buy an imperfect, readily available product from a competitor.

71

	Hand production	Mass production
Primary user concerns	uniqueness, craftsmanship, aesthetic and cultural value	quantity needs, cost constraints, manufacturability
Common materials	wood, leather	aluminum, steel, plastic
Typical number of copies	< 500	> 5,000
Use context	high-end lounges, luxury homes	offices, institutions, airports
Examples	Finn Juhl, Ceccotti Collezioni	IKEA, Knoll

It's hard to make a thousand of something.

Manual production often suits the manufacture of small quantities of an item, such as a few necklaces or a few dozen baskets. **Mass production** suits the making of thousands or millions of an item, but requires substantial up-front investment for planning, training, industrial equipment, and management.

For intermediate quantities of a product, it can be difficult to justify any production method. Manual production can result in uneven quality, high labor costs, and a high retail price for a product that won't be perceived as exclusive. Mass production will reduce direct labor costs, but each item will have to be priced exorbitantly to recoup the up-front investment.

3-D printing and computer numerical control (CNC) technologies can sometimes fill this gap, but the range of products and materials they suit is fairly limited.

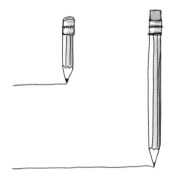

72

The component with the shortest lifespan determines the product lifespan.

In an ideal product life cycle, all components are exhausted at the same time. But most often, one part determines a product's fate. An all-in-one desktop computer, for example, becomes entirely useless when only the monitor fails. In even a simple product such as a hammer, the steel head will long outlast the wood handle.

But products often can be designed to manage component obsolescence. A hammer handle can be designed to be replaceable. A shoe with a glued, molded rubber sole is unlikely to be resoled, suggesting it be designed with a lower quality upper. But a shoe made with the highest quality leather that will last two decades should be paired with a replaceable, welted leather sole.

73

First few uses: emotional
appearance
cool factor
delightful interaction

Extended use: rational
durability
reliability
comfort

Prolonged use: emotional 2.0
life context
familiarity
inner character

Design the user experience through time.

In the first several uses of a product, users may be smitten. Take advantage of their attention by creating early "wow" moments. Electronic products can showcase their personality through lights, sounds, and interface details. A washing machine might display helpful tips and play a happy tune to celebrate the first wash. For physical products, use striking color combinations, precise corner details, and interesting joinery to reward the new user's infatuated gaze.

When a product has been in use for a while, the user may be less interested in quirks and charms. The electronic interface, for example, can be designed to learn and emphasize the user's favorite options and place less-used ones in a submenu. For physical objects, durability and reliability provide the ultimate longtime rewards.

74

"I like the concept of wearing in instead of wearing out."

—BILL MOGGRIDGE, co-founder, IDEO

75

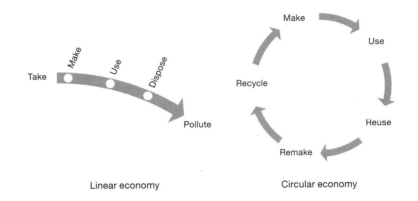

Linear economy

Circular economy

Pollution is a design flaw.

Natural, nonpetroleum-based materials may seem inherently better for the environment. But many items that seem environmentally friendly, from sugar packets to paper cups, are coated with a thin plastic layer, making them difficult and even impossible to recycle. A plastic cup made from a single synthetic material, however, such as polyethylene or polypropylene, can be easily recycled.

76

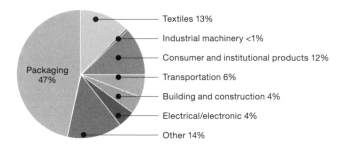

Textiles 13%

Industrial machinery <1%

Consumer and institutional products 12%

Transportation 6%

Building and construction 4%

Electrical/electronic 4%

Other 14%

Packaging
47%

Plastic waste generation by industrial sector, 2015
Source: Roland Geyer, University of California, Santa Barbara

Plastic is a property, not a material.

Plastic describes any material whose shape can be easily changed or molded. Typically, a raw plastic material is shaped in a heated state, then cooled to create a hard or semi-hard product.

The materials we most often refer to as plastic are made from polymers, long chains of carbon and other atoms sourced from petrochemicals. However, plants are being increasingly used as a source. At the end of their service life, **bioplastics** can be consumed by bacteria rather than thrown away.

77

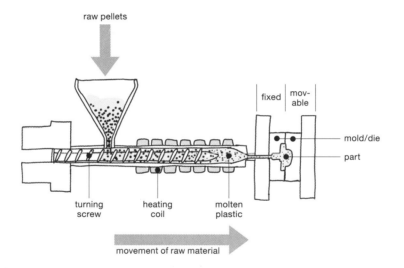

raw pellets

fixed | mov-
able

mold/die

part

turning
screw

heating
coil

molten
plastic

movement of raw material

Injection molding

Many parts are made by heating a raw material, such as plastic pellets, metal, or glass, and injecting it into a metal cavity called a **mold** or **die**. The part is allowed to cool and harden, and is then removed. IM essentials include:

Mold/part shape: A part needs to slide out of its mold after casting. This requires that its sides have a **draft angle** of at least 1°. Additionally, complex shapes with "undercuts" can become trapped in a mold. Side ejection may be possible, but is expensive. Making a part in two pieces will often solve this problem.

Mold or die material: Heat-treated steel "tooling" suits high-volume production, up to 100,000 cycles. Aluminum is less expensive but will last only a few thousand cycles. It is often used for pre-production prototypes that closely resemble the final product.

Production speed: Manufacturing can be accelerated with aluminum tooling, which cools faster but is less durable. Two- or three-cavity molds will produce more units per cycle, increasing initial tooling cost but lowering the cost of each part.

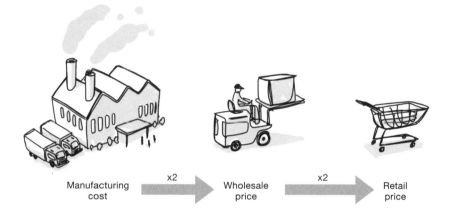

78

Manufacturing
cost

x2 →

Wholesale
price

x2 →

Retail
price

Retail = (BOM + labor) x 4

A **bill of materials** is a detailed list of parts needed to manufacture a product, from motor assemblies to tiny screws. A BOM lists part names, specifications such as dimensions and colors, and their prices. A rough estimate for the retail price of a product, assuming design and development costs are covered within the profit margin, is four times the manufacturing cost.

79

IKEA Poäng chair

The IKEA ecosystem

IKEA is the world's largest furniture company. Fortuitously, it was founded in 1943, as modern sensibilities were moving from the avant-garde to the mainstream. But the biggest reason for IKEA's success is its innovation of an entire product ecosystem.

Complete product line: IKEA, unlike its competitors, makes furniture and accessories for the entire home.

Manufacturing: IKEA manufactures all of its own products.

Retail environment: An immersive, IKEA-only setting serves as both a store and a self-service warehouse.

Low prices: Affordability is realized through high-volume production, selling most products unassembled, and limiting the palette of materials and hardware.

Flat-pack logistics: This is the unifying element in the IKEA system, as it allows customers to transport products home in their vehicles or via public transit.

DIY: Standardized hardware and fasteners foster familiarity and expedite assembly by the user.

Sustainability: Most components are made from a single material, facilitating recycling. IKEA is pursuing 100% reliance on renewable energy for all operations.

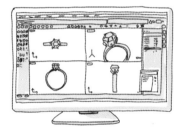

Make important design explorations away from the computer.

The computer is almost always better for refining or generating variations on a concept than for creating or exploring fresh concepts. A concept is holistic; it incorporates many diverse aspects of a project. But a computer image is purely visual and two-dimensional. It lacks context, tactility, volume, weight, temperature, smell, ergonomics, and other qualities one engages when interacting with a physical object.

81

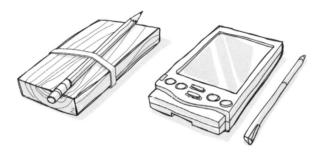

A block of wood served as an early prototype for the smartphone.

Lo-res gets more feedback.

Rough sketches, raw images, and messy prototypes encourage others—
especially non-designers—to become involved in the design process, because
they feel like they can influence the direction of the project. The more carefully
you execute a drawing, the more invested you likely will be in maintaining the design as is, and the less inclined you will be to receive or heed feedback. Computer
renderings, because they tend to display the same degree of polish regardless
of the stage of development, can confuse both non-designers and experienced
designers as to the stage of a project; most often, they suggest a project is more
developed than it really is.

Limit your confidence in a concept to what it has earned.

A concept may deserve your confidence if:

1   It came from a large field of possibilities.

2   You didn't consciously pursue it or see it coming, but it resulted from discoveries during the design process.

3   It is based on real knowledge about the user, has utility, is culturally appropriate, and is technically and economically feasible.

4   It has been validated and improved through testing.

5   Any novelty present is not overpowering. A fitting solution will often seem so obvious that it doesn't seem novel at all.

6   Your confidence is intellectual, not emotional, in nature.

83

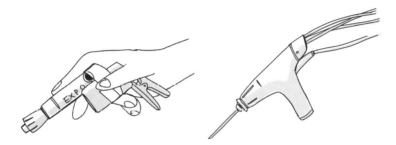

Early mock-up by IDEO to
gain input from surgeons

Completed product

Diego nasal surgery instrument by Gyrus ACMI

Match your craft to your confidence.

Give a drawing, prototype, or other study only as much time, effort, and investment as are needed to generate feedback on the issues relevant at the stage of development. Detail, exactitude, and craft should represent the confidence the design deserves, and no more.

84

It's a Cursor
Control Device.

It's a mouse!

Engineer

Product Designer

The first computer mouse prototype, by Doug Engelbart

You have a concept when you can name it.

A neutral name may objectively and accurately label a concept, but it won't express its core sensibility, foster an emotional connection, or help you keep track of it. You will quickly forget which of your concepts is Concept D and which is Concept M, but you will never confuse your Shark Jaw Concept with your Meek Mole Concept.

When developing and naming a concept, be overly emotive or exaggerated rather than low-key and suggestive, as it's easier to later tamp down an overstatement than juice up an understatement. And don't just use the name as a name; use it to help you make decisions about form, size, materials, and finishes.

85

Conceptual simplicity calls for hidden complexity.

Craighton Berman Studio's Stool No.1 appears to be made from a single, long piece of bent rod. However, this would require a 30' long piece of metal and a cumbersome manufacturing process. Instead, the legs are made from four separate but identical parts that are joined under the seat.

An inexperienced designer may resent such manipulations for "polluting" a design concept. The aware designer understands that **conceptual** or **narrative simplicity** rarely means literal simplicity.

86

Arco lamp
unique scale and pro-
portion extend bound-
ary of floor lamps to that
of suspension lamps

Volkswagen Beetle
ladybug shape

Breuer chair
continuous steel tubing

Apple laptop
monochromatic
elegance

Make one thing more important than everything else.

One clear idea—a design element, quality, shape, function, form, material, color, or feature—should triumph over all others and embody a product's core narrative. Whenever anyone describes the product to the uninitiated, the **Primary Design Component** (PDC) should come up.

Quantitative/numerical

☐ Never
☐ Rarely
☐ Sometimes
☐ Frequently
☐ Always

Qualitative/categorical

Types of data

If you don't have enough answers, you aren't asking enough questions.

When progress is very slow, you may be relying too much on your talents and don't know enough about the user's needs, the product environment, technical considerations, market context, and other factors. When stuck, ask questions about *anything*. If you don't know what color to use, ask questions that aren't directly about color: Where will the product be used? What are its basic physics that affect its use? How will it be manufactured? Will it be used outdoors in the sun as well as indoors? Will it be stored in a drawer or displayed on a coffee table?

Looking inside yourself for answers is important, but looking outside will expand what's inside you. Any time you take in new information, you are unlikely to stay stuck.

88

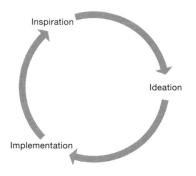

Keep circling back to the elemental questions.

Even when the design process is moving smoothly, it is common to feel that one has not yet identified the core problem to be solved or uncovered the key insight into it.

Structure your design process so that you repeatedly revisit the most basic questions about the undertaking. Rephrase important questions and seek new answers to those already answered. Who is this for? Why do they need it? How and when will they use it? Why did we decide on this form? *Exactly* why?

Your goal should be to make sure that movement toward a solution is grounded in an increasingly better understanding of where you started—or should have started. As you approach the successful conclusion of a project and focus more on details, keep returning to the elemental questions to help you figure out how to execute them.

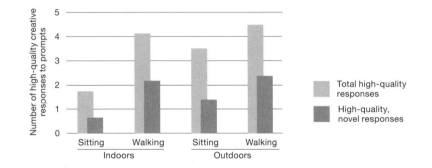

Stanford study on walking and creativity, 2014

More things to do when you're stuck

1 Revisit and rewrite your design statement.
2 Ask new questions about new things you don't necessarily think are relevant to your stuckness. If you ask only what you think you need to ask, you will remain within the same constraints.
3 Reexamine the core motivators of the endeavor to see if your previous answers to *Why?* hold up.
4 Identify assumptions you have made that you didn't have to make. What ideas or values are you married to that you don't have to be married to?
5 Don't just think really hard; do something physical.

There shouldn't be a *ta-da*.

Your instructor or client should be aware of your explorations throughout the design process; there should never be a Big Reveal. If a final presentation surprises, it should be because everything previously explored came together in a delightful, synergistic way.

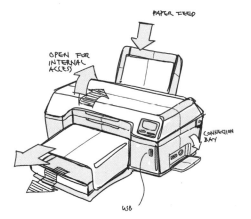

PAPER FEED

OPEN FOR
INTERNAL
ACCESS

CONNECTION
BAY

USB

Indicate the function; don't just show the form.

Draw the hinge in motion, not just the hinge. Show the drawer being opened, not just the drawer. Show the knob being turned, the lid being unscrewed, and the flap swinging open. Show a hand operating a handheld device or flipping a switch. Show the massager vibrating. Draw the chair reclining, the table being unfolded, and the tent being erected. Show the lamp turning on and off.

92

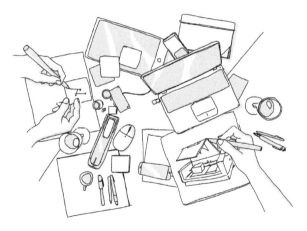

Don't present everything you did.

It is tempting to present all of your drawings and studies to impress reviewers. But this won't help them understand how you viewed the problem, conducted research, evaluated concepts, or arrived at your solution. Curate your material, and present only that which helps you present a coherent narrative. Focus on the key phases of your process, and on convincing the audience that your solution is truly inspired.

Problem
understanding and
framing/reframing of
problem assigned

Process
research/data gathering,
generation and evaluation
of alternatives

Product
quality and
appropriateness of
final solution

Presentation
quality of graphics,
mock-ups, oral
communication

Common categories of evaluation for student projects

Use your critics to your advantage.

Critics visiting the studio often struggle to understand the project assigned, the instructor's intentions, and the relevant issues. Help them figure out what to critique. Identify the focus of the assignment so they don't waste time in the wrong areas. Have a list of questions ready for them to address, instead of merely responding to their criticisms. Highlight things you are struggling to understand or resolve, issues needing further study, and alternative approaches on which you would like coaching.

94

A dead baby whale washed ashore this morning. Inside it was a heap of plastic waste, some of which came from your kitchen.

Story

emphasizes emotions and personal context

We release 1 million tons of plastic waste into the oceans every year. Our five-phase program will solve this problem.

Argument

emphasizes facts, logic, and analysis

Persuade through story, not just argument.

When presenting, begin with a **user-based narrative** on the experiences and pain points of the potential customer. The narrative may be idiosyncratic and focus on a few specific users, but ultimately it should evidence an empathetic understanding of the problem and its context as experienced by many users.

Segue to a **design-based narrative** on how you, the designer, engaged, researched, analyzed, and solved the problem. Discuss your juggling of information and insights, your various design hypotheses, the failures and successes of prototypes, and your arrival at a solution. This narrative should ultimately put forth a logical and convincing argument.

Return to and synthesize the user narrative. Show how your solution addresses the user's pain points and how it will naturally insinuate itself into the user's life context.

Made in	China	Chicago
Retail price	$350	$35
Process	welded, injection molded, assembled	cut, sewn
Materials	steel, plastic, electronics	leather, thread
Minimum order	1,000	50
Shipping cost	$40	$8

Make your first product small and light.

Self-launching a new product is often a designer's first business endeavor. A simple product is best; even if unsuccessful, you will learn more about engineering, presentation, sourcing, production, marketing, shipping, and customer service than you will through a well-considered conceptual project.

Choose a product that is inexpensive to manufacture and easy to ship. A product that requires a large production start-up, such as an injection-molded phone case, is riskier than a wallet that can be produced in small quantities at a reasonable per-unit price. Large, heavy objects, such as furniture, will incur high shipping and inventory costs.

Copyright
usu. valid for 50
to 70 years after
death of creator

**U.S. Registered
Trademark**
may be valid indefinitely

TM

Trademark
not registered;
may or may not
be protectable

Utility patent
20 years

Design patent
15 years

Nondisclosure agreement
Protects ideas shown to potential
partners and investors

Intellectual property protection

Use a patent to protect your business interest, not your emotional interest.

Creations are personal; protecting them through registration with the US Patent and Trademark Office might seem like a way to safeguard one's emotional investment in them. But the real benefit of intellectual property (IP) protection is economic.

A **utility patent** grants a creator legal ownership of a functional improvement to a product, process, technology, or mechanism. It can be costly, but if granted by the USPTO the patent holder may legally prevent competitors from copying or using the improvement, charge or license others for its use, or sell it outright.

A **design patent** protects aesthetic or ornamental elements rather than function. It is easier to obtain than a utility patent but may be difficult to protect, as competitors can market very similar designs.

A **provisional patent** temporarily prevents others from using a creation for which one has filed a patent application, pending approval or rejection by the USPTO.

97

Platform	Content	Exposure	Target audience
Online portfolio / Website	Full project detail	Low	Industry professionals
Social media	Single image or glimpse of project	High	Personal network, general public
Design competition	Full project detail	Low to medium	Industry professionals

People you don't know at all may be more helpful than those you know well.

In seeking professional connections, job interviews, clients, and social connections, it is natural to lean on people we know well: friends, family, schoolmates, professors, and co-workers. But the longer you have known someone, the more likely it is that you have already benefited from the connections and opportunities they can provide. Strangers and near strangers—people you don't know personally but with whom you share a common contact—have entirely different social and professional networks that may be rife with new possibilities.

98

Commercial
product designer

User Interface/User
Experience designer

Exhibit designer

Technician

Designer-entrepreneur

Design researcher

Product design careers

Your first job only needs to be your first job.

You are unlikely to know early in your career which areas of product design you will be best at, which will have market longevity, and which will maintain your interest.

There's no right place to start. Gain experience in as many different areas as you can. Work outside your comfort zone. Get good at many things, not one thing. When you find the one thing you want to do, everything that came before will inform and enrich it.

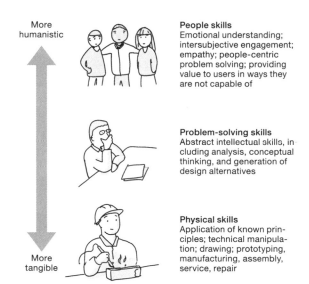

People skills
Emotional understanding; intersubjective engagement; empathy; people-centric problem solving; providing value to users in ways they are not capable of

Problem-solving skills
Abstract intellectual skills, including analysis, conceptual thinking, and generation of design alternatives

Physical skills
Application of known principles; technical manipulation; drawing; prototyping, manufacturing, assembly, service, repair

More humanistic

More tangible

The skills totem

The ultimate skill isn't a design skill; it's the skill of understanding.

School typically focuses on developing students' physical and intellectual skills, which may imply that these will produce a fully realized, star designer. But the most advanced skill a professional designer can have is the ability to read and interpret people and, with modesty and empathy, know what they need or want better than they themselves know.

100

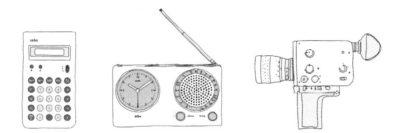

Products designed by Dieter Rams

Your work will look like you even if you don't try to make it look like you.

Self-expression, to the extent it has a place in design, does not come from pursuing an outcome you think is "you." It comes from investigating a problem as honestly, sensitively, and thoroughly as possible, and making the most appropriate decision in each circumstance, whether or not you think it expresses who you are. Whatever results when you are not trying to be you is that which is most inescapably you.

NOTES

Lesson 33: "Pete Pinnell: Thoughts on Cups." https://www.youtube.com/1watch?v=WChFMMzLHVs, accessed December 5, 2019.

Lesson 90: Marily Oppezzo and Daniel L. Schwartz, "Give Your Ideas Some Legs: The Positive Effect of Walking on Creative Thinking," *Journal of Experimental Psychology: Learning, Memory, and Cognition*, American Psychological Association, vol. 40, no. 4 (2014): 1142–1152.

Index

[3-D printing, 25
5E customer journey, 2

affordances, 28
Alessi (houseware design company), 35
Anna G. corkscrew, 35
Apple,
    iPod, 11
    laptop, 87
archetypes, 9
Arco lamp, 87
art, modern versus traditional, 38

B&B Italia (furniture company), 35
beauty, 26
bill of materials (BOM), 79
brainstorming, 13, 14, 20
brand expansion, 6
Brembo brake caliper, 57
Breuer chair, 87
Breuer, Marcel (designer/architect), 67
buttons and switches, 53, 68, 69, 70

Camel table, 29
camera, 25, 38, 46

careers for product designers, 96, 98, 99, 100
Carlton room divider, 35
Casio, 27
Ceccotti Collezioni (furniture/design company), 72
chairs/seating, 66, 67
Christianson, Linda (potter), 33
Ciscotti, Biagio (architect and designer), 35
cleverness, 34
Colombo, Joe Cesare (designer), 30
color, material, and finish (CMF) see also materials, 59, 60, 61, 62, 63, 64
computer mouse, 85
computer numerical control (CNC) milling, 25, 72
core products/core experience, 6
cost of products, 79
Craighton Berman Studio (design firm), 86
creativity/originality/self-expression, 7, 10, 12, 14, 90, 101

data, types of, 88
design concept, 12, 13, 14, 15, 17, 20, 22, 85, 86, 87
design process, 1, 22, 24, 43, 64, 81, 82, 83, 84, 88, 89, 90, 91, 101
design team, 23
The Design of Everyday Things (book), 67
details, 53, 54, 55, 56, 57, 58, 60, 61
Diabolix bottle opener, 35
Diego nasal surgery instrument 84
dissonance, as a design value, 33
drawing, 7, 13, 39, 40, 41, 42, 65, 82, 92
Duchamp, Marcel, 38
Dyson products, 58

economy, linear vs. circular, 76
elegance, versus extravagance, 32
empathy, and sympathy, 19
Engelbart, Doug (engineer/inventor), 85

environment, natural, 76, 77, 80
ergonomics, 1, 48, 65, 81
extravagance, versus elegance, 32
eyeglasses, 31

feedback, for product user, 70
form, and shape, 25, 30, 31, 32, 35
Fountain (artwork by Marcel Duchamp), 38
Freitag bag, 17

GAF View-Master, 49
Gandhi, Mahatma , 31
gender, accommodating in design, 18
gimmickry, 34, 35
Gyrus ACMI (medical devices company), 84

Harrison, Charles (designer), 49
Honeywell thermostat, 9

IDEO (design consulting firm) 75, 84
injection molding, 77, 78
Ive, Jonathan (designer), 11

Jaywayne humidifier, 5
Jobs, Steve, 31

Juhl, Finn (architect and designer), 72
Juicy Salif lemon juicer, 35

IDEO (design consulting firm), 75
IKEA (furniture/design company), 72, 80
intellectual property protection, 97

Keeley, Larry (design strategist), 2
kitsch, 35, 37
Knoll (office furniture company), 72

Lego, 34, 46
Lennon, John, 31
lifespan/life cycle, of products, 73, 74, 75, 76
Loewy, Raymond (industrial designer), 10

MacArthur, Douglas, 31
Manufacturing/production, 25, 46, 64, 72, 78, 79, 80, 83, 86, 100
materials, 49, 59, 63, 64, 72, 77, 78
  see also Color, material, and finish (CMF)
MAYA principle, 10

Memphis Milano (architecture and design firm), 35
Mendini, Alessandro (architect and designer), 35
mock-ups/models/prototypes, 42, 43, 48, 82, 84, 85, 100
modernism, 24, 32, 38 , 80
modular products, 46
Moggridge, Bill (co-founder, IDEO), 75
Mold-Tech, 64
Moore, Patricia (designer) , 19

nature, emulating, 29
Nest thermostat, 9
Neutra, Richard (designer), 29
Noguchi, Isamu (designer), 52
Norman, Donald (design researcher), 67

originality/creativity/self-expression, 7, 10, 12, 14, 90, 101

Pantone, 64
Patek Philippe, 27
Pesce, Gaetano (architect and designer), 35
Pinnell, Pete (potter), 33
plastics, 76, 77, 78
portability, 44
pottery, 33, 55
presentation, 91, 92, 93, 94, 95

Primary Design Component (PDC), 87
problem
    identifying/framing/reframing, 3, 4, 5, 16, 17
    solving within systems, 2, 8
product designer, defined, 23
product housing, 54
product personality, 21
product systems, 2, 8, 80

RGB versus CMYK (color selection), 64
Radio Flyer, 36
Rams, Dieter (industrial designer), 101
Rashid, Karim (designer), 30
recycling, 17, 44, 76, 77, 80

screw heads, 56
secondary products, 6
self-expression/creativity/originality, 7, 10, 12, 14, 90, 101
sign value, 27, 30
Sisifo lamp, 10
smartphone, 1, 82
The Social Life of Small Urban Spaces (book), 16
software, 71
Sottsass, Ettore (architect and designer), 35
stability of products, 50, 55
Starck, Philippe (designer), 35
sustainability, 76, 77, 80
sympathy, and empathy, 19

Taj Mahal, 26
toys, 36

Up lounger, 35
use modes, 45
users,
    experience, 1, 2, 6, 9, 10, 23, 28, 68, 70, 74, 84, 99
    motivations and needs, 4, 5, 6, 19
utility value, 27

Velcro, 29
ventilation, 55, 58
virtual/digital interface, 1, 23
Volkswagen, 68, 87

Wassily chair, 67
weight/gravity, 50, 51, 52
Whyte, William H., 16
Wilson, Scott (designer), 10
Writing, as a design tool, 13, 15, 90

Sung Jang is an artist, industrial designer, principal of Sung Jang Laboratory, and associate professor of industrial design at the University of Illinois at Chicago.

Martin Thaler practices globally as a product design consultant and is a studio professor at the Institute of Design, Illinois Institute of Technology.

Matthew Frederick is an architect, urban designer, instructor of design and writing, and the creator of the acclaimed 101 Things I Learned® series. He lives in New York's Hudson Valley.